FRANKLIN *Pierce*

FRANKLIN *Pierce*

OUR FOURTEENTH PRESIDENT

By Steven Ferry

SPIRIT
of America™

The Child's World®, Inc.
Chanhassen, Minnesota

FRANKLIN *Pierce*

Published in the United States of America by The Child's World®, Inc.
PO Box 326 • Chanhassen, MN 55317-0326 • 800-599-READ • www.childsworld.com

Acknowledgments
The Creative Spark: Mary Francis-DeMarois, Project Director; Elizabeth Sirimarco Budd, Series Editor; Robert Court, Design and Art Direction; Janine Graham, Page Layout; Jennifer Moyers, Production

The Child's World®, Inc.: Mary Berendes, Publishing Director; Red Line Editorial, Fact Research; Cindy Klingel, Curriculum Advisor; Robert Noyed, Historical Advisor

Photos
Cover: p. 34: White House Collection, courtesy White House Historical Association; Bowdoin College Museum of Art: 9; Bowdoin College Special Collections: 8; Chicago Historical Society: 30; The Granger Collection, New York, 27, 29; Library of Congress 7, 11, 16, 18, 20, 22, 23, 25, 26, 28, 32, 37; New Hampshire Historical Society: 12, 13, 21; Courtesy of the Pierce Brigade, Concord, NH (David M. Budd Photography): 6, 14, 15, 35, 36; Stock Montage: 31

Library of Congress Cataloging-in-Publication Data
Ferry, Steven, 1953–
    Franklin Pierce : our fourteenth president / by Steven Ferry.
        p. cm.
    Includes bibliographical references (p.) and index.
    ISBN 1-56766-851-8 (library bound : alk. paper)
    1. Pierce, Franklin, 1804–1869—Juvenile literature. 2.Presidents—United States—Biography—
Juvenile literature. [1. Pierce, Franklin, 1804–1869. 2. Presidents.] I. Title.
    E432 .F47 2001
    973.6'6'092--dc21
                                                                00-011453

15   27   32

Contents

Chapter ONE

A Promising Start

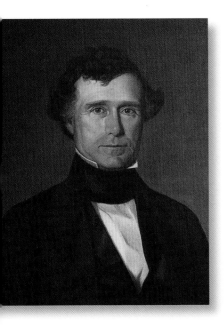

Franklin Pierce, nicknamed "Handsome Frank," was elected president in 1852. He was 47 years old and the youngest man to be elected president up to that time.

FRANKLIN PIERCE, THE 14TH U.S. PRESIDENT, was born in Hillsborough, New Hampshire. His father, Benjamin, was one of the town's earliest settlers. As a young man, Benjamin joined the army to help America win its independence from Great Britain. After nine years of war, he returned to Hillsborough as a hero of the **Revolution.** He soon married Anna Kendrick. Over their years together, Benjamin and Anna had eight children. Franklin was their sixth child, born on November 23, 1804.

Like his brothers and sisters before him, Franklin was born in a small log cabin. But soon after his birth, the family moved to a spacious house that Benjamin had built for them. As a young boy of eight years old, Franklin listened to exciting stories about the

War of 1812. Two of his older brothers had joined the American army, just as their father had years before. Franklin hoped to one day serve his country, too. He often listened to his father give speeches in support of President Madison and the war. As he grew older, he would remember his father's belief in **democracy.**

Benjamin Pierce did not have the advantage of a good education. But he insisted that

The Pierces' family home was located three miles outside of Hillsborough, New Hampshire. Pierce is the only president to have been born in that state.

7

Young Franklin Pierce made friends easily and wanted people to like him. He was also full of mischief, pulling pranks and picking fights whenever he could. This silhouette of him was made while he was a college student.

his sons should have the best schooling possible. Franklin began attending school as a young boy and soon learned to read. He was a fast learner and often helped tutor other students during recess.

By age 16, he was ready for college and enrolled at Bowdoin (pronounced BOW-dun) College in Brunswick, Maine.

At first, Franklin's grades were not very good. He often skipped classes to spend time with his friends. Luckily, two classmates convinced him to try harder. For three months, Franklin woke up at four o'clock each morning and then studied until midnight. He became such a good student that he taught classes at a small schoolhouse during his vacation.

By the time Pierce graduated from Bowdoin in 1824, he was one of the best students in his class. He decided to study law. In September of 1827, he passed his law exams and became a lawyer. That same year, his father was elected governor of New Hampshire. Pierce soon decided to follow in his father's footsteps. He began his own career in **politics.** In 1829, Franklin Pierce was elected to his first political office. He was just 24 years old when he became a **representative**

Pierce graduated from Bowdoin College, below, in 1824. Many important people have graduated from Bowdoin in addition to President Pierce. Its first black student, John Brown Russwurm, started the first newspaper for African Americans. Robert Peary, the first explorer to reach the North Pole, graduated from the school in 1877.

to the New Hampshire legislature. A legislature is the part of a government that makes laws.

Both Franklin Pierce and his father were members of the Democratic Party. This **political party** was founded by President Andrew Jackson and his friends. The Democrats promised to protect the rights of ordinary Americans. They also wanted to keep the **federal** government from gaining too much power. The Democrats believed the states should be able to make laws for themselves.

Pierce remained in the state legislature for four years. He served as the speaker of the house, the leader who takes charge of the meetings. He was also the head of the education committee. In 1832, New Hampshire voters elected Pierce to the U.S. Congress. He moved to Washington, D.C., and served as a representative for four years.

For many years, problems had been brewing between the Northern and Southern states. Many Northerners believed slavery should be stopped. But Southerners depended on slave labor to run their large farms, called plantations. While Pierce was in Congress, the situation grew worse. Although he was from the North, Pierce did not believe that slavery should be **abolished.** Instead, he thought the states should decide for themselves whether to allow it. He thought the best way for the **Union** to stay together was for the North and the South to compromise. This meant that both sides would have to give up part of what they wanted in order to reach an agreement. Throughout Pierce's career, slavery would be the most important issue facing the nation.

Soon after moving to Washington, Pierce married Jane Means Appleton. Unfortunately, the couple would have a difficult life together. Jane was a quiet, shy woman who was very religious. Franklin was fun-loving and outgoing. He was a man who loved to attend parties and meet new people. Jane disapproved of drinking alcohol, but her husband enjoyed meeting his friends at a local tavern for drinks and conversation.

Franklin's personality made him popular in Washington, and he was a success in politics. But Jane hated politics and life in the capital city.

Nathaniel Hawthorne was one of Pierce's closest friends. They met at college. Hawthorne later became a well-known author. He wrote The Scarlet Letter *and other famous novels, but he also wrote Pierce's biography (the story of Pierce's life).*

Jane Pierce was a shy girl whose father had been president of Bowdoin College before Pierce enrolled there. She met her future husband after he graduated from Bowdoin, when he was a young lawyer who wanted to enter politics.

Jane tried many times to convince Franklin to leave Washington, but he always refused. The couple often quarreled. Still, Pierce tried to be kind and loving to his wife. Finally, Jane returned to New Hampshire. In 1836, she had their first child, Franklin Jr. Sadly, the baby died when he was just three days old. It was the first of many personal tragedies that would haunt the Pierces throughout their lives together.

12

IN 1829, PIERCE MOVED TO CONCORD, NEW HAMPSHIRE, TO SERVE ON THE state legislature. At first he stayed at a boarding house, paying the owner 50¢ a day. Many out-of-town legislators stayed in boarding houses. It was much cheaper than taking a room at the Eagle Coffee House (shown above), a local inn that cost $1 a day. But the Eagle was closer to the State House, and many legislators would have preferred to stay there.

When Pierce became the speaker of the house, he received a raise in pay. The legislature now paid him $2.50 a day. He could afford to stay at the Eagle Coffee House. How did he spend the rest of his money during his first term? He bought seven bottles of wine for $1 each and many 3¢ cigars. He spent 50¢ when he needed to get his "boots blacked" (his shoes shined). It cost $3.40 to board his horse for 17 nights and another $4.90 for the three bushels of oats the horse ate.

Chapter TWO

Life in Politics

Although Pierce was a good speaker, he rarely gave speeches as a member of Congress. He preferred to speak only when he had something important to say. He let more experienced lawmakers do most of the talking.

PIERCE WAS ELECTED TO THE U.S. SENATE in 1836. He almost always voted with the Democratic Party, only voting against it once. Some Democrats wanted to make a rule that would stop senators from suggesting new laws about slavery. Pierce was against this. He felt that people who were against slavery, called **abolitionists,** should be able to express their views. If they were not, it might cause even more problems between the North and the South. Other than this, Pierce was always loyal to his party.

Meanwhile, Jane Pierce was raising their second son, Frank Robert, in New Hampshire. She had been living there without Franklin for some time. She yearned for her husband to return to his family, especially after their third son, Benjamin, was born. Pierce gave up his Senate seat in 1842 and began practicing law in Concord, New Hampshire. This made his wife happy, but her happiness was short-lived. Frank Robert, who was only four years old, died in 1843. It was another sad time for the Pierces.

Pierce did not leave politics completely, but he made sure he stayed close to Jane and Benjamin by only taking part in local politics.

After the Pierces' second son died, Jane became very protective of their son Benjamin, whom they called Bennie. She made sure that he had strict religious training. He attended family worship every morning, said prayers every evening, and went to church with his parents on Sundays. He also listened to his mother tell Bible stories and sang hymns with her.

The nation's political leaders did not forget him, though. President James Polk named Pierce the district attorney of New Hampshire in 1845. This meant he was in charge of the state's legal matters. The following year, the president asked Pierce to join his cabinet, the group of people who helped him make important decisions. This would have meant returning to Washington, D.C., and Pierce knew Jane would never agree to it.

Pierce wrote to Polk, turning down the offer. "Although the early years of my manhood were devoted to public life," he wrote, "it was never really suited to my taste. I longed … for the quiet and independence that belong only to the private citizen." Pierce said that when he left the Senate, he promised never to leave his family again. He told the president that nothing could change his mind—unless the nation went to war.

And that is exactly what happened. In 1846, like his father and brothers before him, Pierce joined the army to fight for his country. The United States was at war with Mexico, battling for control of Texas. Pierce entered the army as a private, the lowest rank of soldier. The following year, he was a brigadier general, in charge of 2,500 soldiers.

Pierce set sail for the port town of Vera Cruz, Mexico, in May 1847. That July, he led his troops on the march to Mexico City. He was not very useful as a soldier, however. He was knocked unconscious in battle when he was thrown from his horse. In another battle, he twisted his knee and fainted again. Even though he had stomach problems and saddle blisters, he stayed with the army until it captured Mexico City in September of 1847.

Pierce resigned from the army in 1848 and returned home. New Hampshire residents welcomed him as a hero, but Pierce was disappointed. He had hoped to gain glory as a soldier. He felt he had let down himself and his country. He returned to practicing law and lived quietly in Concord with his wife and son.

▶ Winning the
Mexican War caused
problems for the
United States.
The nation had to
decide whether to
allow slavery in the
new territories
it had acquired.

Perhaps life would have been good to the Pierce family if Franklin had stuck to his decision to stay out of national politics. But he did not. The Democrats were unable to agree on a presidential **candidate** in 1852. After 34 **ballots,** no one had won the **nomination.**

Pierce was eager to serve his country during the Mexican War. He did not have great success as a soldier, however.

18

Finally, some of Pierce's friends suggested that he would be a good candidate. Jane Pierce was so upset when she heard the news that she fainted.

It took 15 more ballots before the Democrats nominated Pierce. But they did not choose him because they believed he would be a good leader—they simply couldn't agree on anyone else! Southerners voted for Pierce because he approved of slavery in the South. Northerners voted for him because he had done so little in politics, he hadn't made any enemies.

The presidential election that followed was between Pierce and his former commander during the war, General Winfield Scott. Scott and his supporters said many nasty things about Pierce during the **campaign.** For one thing, Scott said that Pierce had acted like a coward during the Mexican War. The Democrats fought back by telling people that Pierce had always been a strong supporter of popular President Jackson. They called him "Young Hickory," reminding voters of Andrew Jackson's nickname, "Old Hickory."

Pierce was a pleasant man who liked to meet and talk with people. He was able to remember names and faces. He promised favors to people if they elected him. After a close election, Pierce became the new president.

Unfortunately, things went wrong before he even took office. In January of 1853, the Pierces were traveling by train when tragedy struck again. There was a terrible accident. Young Benjamin, the Pierces' only living son, was killed before his parents' eyes.

JANE PIERCE NEVER WANTED HER husband to be president. She had always hated politics and wanted to lead a quiet life. A solemn and serious woman, Jane did not like the social life of a politician's wife. She felt it demanded a cheerful disposition and a love of parties, neither of which she had.

After the Pierce's first two sons died, Jane focused all her attention on Bennie. After his death, she refused to accompany her husband to Washington. She did not think she could bear life in the nation's capital. In fact, she felt certain that God had taken Bennie so that her husband would have fewer things on his mind when he became president. Pierce entered the presidency alone and under a cloud of great sorrow. His wife's behavior upset him even more. He began to think of Bennie's death as punishment for his faults.

Jane Pierce later joined her husband in Washington. For the first two years of the presidency, Jane rarely left her living quarters at the White House. She went out only to attend church. She left the hostess duties of the first lady to a friend, preferring to pray and write sad letters to her dead son. People began to call her the "shadow of the White House."

Finally, in 1855, Jane began to appear at her husband's side when guests visited the White House. Although she always greeted people with a smile, visitors said that her face still bore the signs of grief. One guest recalled his visit to the White House with these words, "Everything in that mansion seems cold and cheerless. I have seen hundreds of log cabins which seemed to contain more happiness."

Chapter THREE

An Unhappy President

Pierce's term was a sad time, both for him and for the nation. While Pierce mourned the loss of his son, slavery threatened to tear the nation in two.

SO BEGAN PIERCE'S PRESIDENCY. BOTH HE AND his wife were devastated by the loss of their son. Jane Pierce collapsed with grief. She was too upset to go with her husband to Washington. Pierce's **inauguration** took place on a gray and snowy day that must have mirrored the president's mood. He could scarcely face the huge responsibility of the presidency after the tragedy.

"You have summoned me in my weakness," Pierce said in his inaugural address on March 4, 1853. He asked Americans to support him with their strength. He also spoke of how well America was doing and how it should continue to grow peacefully. He promised to protect the rights of the states that were guaranteed by the **Constitution**—

UNCLE TOM'S CABIN

TOPSY.

In 1852, author Harriet Beecher Stowe wrote a book called Uncle Tom's Cabin. *It showed slaves as real people for the first time. Many Americans finally realized how cruel slavery was. While living in Ohio, just north of the slave state of Kentucky, Stowe and her family were a part of the Underground Railroad. This was the secret route for slaves escaping to the North. To write the book, Stowe used the information she learned from the slaves who stayed at her house. Later* Uncle Tom's Cabin *became a stage play.*

including slavery. He said that the issue of slavery would not destroy the Union.

Pierce had some success as president. He set about expanding the Union, as he had promised to do at his inauguration. He ordered the purchase of land from Mexico

▶ Franklin Pierce was
the first president to
give his inauguration
speech from memory,
without reading
from notes.

▶ Pierce is the only
president who kept all
the members of his
cabinet throughout
his term.

▶ Pierce was the first
president to have
central heating in the
White House.

▶ In 1854, Pierce was
the first president to
have a Christmas tree
in the White House.

for $10 million. This would add thousands of square miles to Arizona and New Mexico so the United States could build a southern railroad to the Pacific Ocean. This became known as the Gadsden Purchase, named for the American official who was in charge of it. It created the official border between Mexico and the United States. Pierce also signed a **treaty** that allowed U.S. fishermen to fish in the waters off Canada. In return, the Canadians could sell their products in the United States without paying taxes.

Another important feat during Pierce's presidency was begun by the president before him, Millard Fillmore. Since early in the 17th century, Japan had usually refused to allow Americans and Europeans into the country. President Fillmore wanted to open trade with Japan, so he sent U.S. Navy Commodore Matthew Perry there with four ships. Perry finally arrived in Yedo Bay in July of 1853, shortly after Pierce became president. Commander Perry gave the Japanese a letter from Fillmore, requesting that the Japanese consider trading with the United States. In March of 1854, Perry and the Japanese signed a treaty of peace and friendship that opened trade between the two countries.

After the Gadsden Purchase, Pierce wanted to increase the size of the nation even more. He tried to convince the British to give the United States part of the coast of Central America. But this did not make all Americans happy. It angered many Northerners because slavery would be legal in the region. They believed Pierce was trying not only to increase the size of the nation, but also the number of **slave states.**

The same disagreements arose about Cuba. Southerners wanted this island to become part of the United States. They believed its sugar plantations and slave trade could help slavery survive and expand. Pierce and his assistants, who were all Southerners, decided to offer the Spanish $130 million for Cuba. They threatened that if Spain did not accept the offer, the United States would take Cuba by force.

Commander Perry and Japanese officials signed an important treaty in 1854. The Japanese agreed to open their ports to American ships. They also promised to protect American sailors who were shipwrecked in Japan and to provide coal for American ships traveling to China.

When Northerners learned of the plan, they were furious. They claimed the plan to take over Cuba was just another way to strengthen slavery in the nation. Pierce and the Southerners had to give up their idea. Northerners accused Pierce of siding with the pro-slavery South.

The battle over slavery was soon to grow more fierce. In May of 1854, Congress passed the Kansas-Nebraska Act. Kansas and Nebraska had been free **territories** since the Missouri Compromise of 1820, which had made slavery illegal in regions north of Missouri. But the new act allowed settlers in

Kansas and Nebraska to decide for themselves whether to allow slavery.

With the new law, the country began arguing about slavery again. Many abolitionists went to live in Kansas. They believed that if more people who hated slavery lived there, they would have a better chance of turning the territory against it. People who were in favor of slavery did the same thing.

Fighting soon broke out in Kansas. The situation grew worse when supporters of slavery won the vote to make Kansas a slave territory. Slavery supporters had cast 6,300 votes, but there were only 1,500 of them living in the area. Abolitionists learned that about 4,000 pro-slavery voters had traveled to Kansas from Missouri to cast the illegal votes.

The Kansas legislature was in favor of slavery. It refused to allow a new vote. To fight back, abolitionists set up their own government. Pierce did not take time to hear both

Between 1830 and 1850, millions of people came to live in the United States from other countries. A new political party, the Nativists, was formed in 1843. The Nativist Party's goal was to keep "America for the Americans." They wanted to prevent immigrants from other countries from voting, holding public office, or becoming citizens. The party created trouble during Pierce's presidency. In 1855, a Nativist mob killed 20 immigrants in Kentucky, claiming that German and Irish immigrants had attacked other Americans who had tried to vote.

sides of the story. Instead, he said the abolitionist government was a form of **rebellion.** He ordered it to disband and sent troops to enforce his decision. Northerners now believed Pierce was firmly in favor of slavery.

Pierce's actions did not help matters. In fact, problems grew worse when the abolitionists would not give up. In the spring of 1856, a **civil war** broke out in the territory. Pro-slavery forces broke into the homes of abolitionists and burned down buildings.

John Brown was a fierce abolitionist who moved to Kansas to keep it from becoming a slave territory. He was accused of murdering five pro-slavery men on May 24, 1856.

Abolitionist John Brown decided to fight back by organizing a brutal attack on his pro-slavery neighbors. Brown and six other men, including his four sons, broke into several cabins and murdered five men. Soon, warfare was raging throughout the territory. By the time peace was reached, more than 200 people had been killed. Americans began calling the territory "Bleeding Kansas."

THE VIOLENCE OF 1856 WAS NOT LIMITED TO THE STATE OF KANSAS. BATTLES even took place in Congress. In May, Representative Preston Brooks of South Carolina attacked Senator Charles Sumner from Massachusetts. Sumner had given a bitter, dramatic speech against people who supported slavery. He even insulted some of the other senators. The speech was later called "The Crime Against Kansas."

When Brooks heard about the speech, he was furious. He rushed onto the Senate floor and found Sumner seated at his desk. Brooks beat Sumner brutally with his cane until Sumner collapsed to the floor, bleeding.

Some members of Congress tried to get Brooks removed from the House. Northerners declared that Brooks's actions went against the right to freedom of speech that is promised by the Constitution. But many people from the South were proud of his actions. In fact, Brooks won the next election by unanimous vote, which means he received every vote. It took Sumner more than three years to heal from his injuries, and Northerners left his seat empty as a symbol of the attack upon him.

29

Chapter FOUR

A Sad Ending

Pierce hoped that the Democrats would select him as their candidate in 1856. But they did not believe he had the strength to lead the country during such a difficult time.

AFTER THE PROBLEMS IN KANSAS, THE Democrats lost faith in President Pierce. Still, near the end of his term, Pierce felt he could claim "a peaceful condition of things in Kansas." He hoped the Democrats would choose him as their candidate in the next election. But his party did not think he could win the election because he had failed to stop the fighting in Kansas. They also felt that in such a troubled time, Pierce could not provide the leadership the nation needed. They chose James Buchanan as the Democratic candidate. To the relief of Mrs. Pierce, she and Franklin would soon be leaving the White House.

When President Buchanan took office, the Pierces left Washington. They began a long tour of Europe, the West Indies, and the United

States. Mrs. Pierce's health had grown worse during her husband's presidency. Franklin Pierce hoped the travel would improve her health and cheer her up. She was still grieving the loss of her children and carried Bennie's Bible with her wherever she went. Finally, in 1860, they returned to Concord to be near family and friends. They had been away for three years.

By this time, the disagreements over slavery between the North and the South were bringing the country ever closer to civil war.

John Brown and his supporters continued to fight slavery after President Pierce left office. In 1859, they tried to raid an arsenal, a place that held a supply of government weapons. They planned to use the weapons to start a slave rebellion. Brown and 21 of his followers captured the arsenal, but they were unable to escape. Soldiers captured Brown, and he was later hung for treason—a crime against the government.

"I wish I [had] higher hope for the future of our country," said Pierce after he arrived home. "But the aspect of any vision is fearfully dark."

Like Pierce, President Buchanan could do nothing to solve the conflict during his four years in office. In fact, many Americans felt that he, too, had made the situation worse. Democrats would not nominate Buchanan as their candidate for the election of 1860. But no matter what, it seemed the Democrats were destined to lose the election.

That November, Abraham Lincoln was elected president. Unlike Pierce and Buchanan,

Lincoln was a member of the Republican Party, which opposed the spread of slavery. Most of all, Lincoln wanted to hold the United States together at any cost. Unfortunately, Southern states were convinced Lincoln would immediately outlaw slavery once he entered office. Soon after he was elected, they began to **secede** from the Union. By April 12, 1861, the nation was at war.

When the Civil War began, Pierce was a bitter foe of President Lincoln and his supporters. He criticized the Union for its actions during the war. He wrote to an old friend, saying, "If I were in the Southerners' places, after so many years of aggression, I should probably be doing what they are doing." Such talk made Pierce unpopular in New Hampshire. He lost many of his friends and supporters, who believed he was a **traitor.**

To add to his sorrow, Jane died in 1863. Although their marriage had sometimes been difficult, he had always loved her very much and tried to do as she wished. Jane Pierce was buried near her children's graves at the Old North Cemetery in Concord.

Pierce spent his last years alone. He had not touched a drop of alcohol for more than 20 years, in part to please Jane. But he began to drink heavily after her death. His health eventually began to fail during the summer of 1869. He died on October 8 and was buried next to his wife and children.

Franklin Pierce has not gone down in history as a good president. He entered the

Pierce said many times that Lincoln made bad decisions and created more problems during the Civil War. Most people did not like to hear Pierce speak against the president. Many Northerners believed Lincoln was a great leader who would save the Union.

presidency during one of the most difficult periods in U.S. history, when Americans had to decide the future of slavery. He was not able to solve the problem, and things grew worse while he was president. But Pierce was an honest man who wanted to uphold the Constitution. His old friend Nathaniel Hawthorne once wrote that Pierce "has in him many of the chief elements of a great ruler." Unfortunately, President Pierce was not able to live up to such great hopes.

Pierce moved into this home in Concord shortly after he left his post as a U.S. senator. Today it is a National Historic Site. The house has been restored so that it is much as it would have been when Pierce, his wife, and their sons lived there. Much of its furniture and decorations belonged to the Pierces.

36

PIERCE WAS RAISED AN EPISCOPALIAN but was a bit lazy about practicing his faith as a young man. During his last year at Bowdoin College, this changed. He prayed every night with a friend. When he married Jane, she insisted that they read the Bible and say their prayers each day. But while he lived away from home, Pierce did not practice his religion so faithfully.

Later, when their third son died, Pierce began to think his children had been taken from him as punishment for ignoring religion. "We should have lived for God," he wrote in his diary, "and have left the dear ones to the care of Him who is alone able to take care of them and us." Pierce began to attend church regularly. As the president, he read prayers each day, said grace at each meal, and was so strict about not working on Sunday that he even refused to read his mail. Many members of the White House staff went to church out of respect for the president and first lady.

Pierce drifted away from the church again after his wife's death in 1863. But after a severe illness the next year, he became active with his church again. When he died in 1869, Pierce had made his peace with God. He believed that after death, he would go on to a better life. The photograph at left is of his tomb at the Old North Cemetery in Concord.

1804 Franklin Pierce is born in Hillsborough, New Hampshire, on November 23.

1824 Pierce graduates from Bowdoin College, in Brunswick, Maine.

1827 Pierce begins to practice law in New Hampshire.

1829 New Hampshire elects Pierce to the state legislature. He holds the post until 1833.

1831 Pierce is elected speaker of the house of the New Hampshire State legislature. He is the youngest man to serve in this post.

1832 Pierce is elected a U.S. congressman. He holds the post for four years.

1834 Pierce marries Jane Means Appleton on November 10.

1836 Franklin Jr., the Pierces' first son, is born. He dies three days later. New Hampshire elects Pierce as a U.S. senator. He holds the position until 1842.

1839 The Pierces' second son, Frank Robert, is born.

1841 The Pierces' third son, Benjamin (Bennie), is born.

1842 Pierce leaves the U.S. Senate to return home to his family.

1843 Frank Robert Pierce dies.

1845 President Polk names Pierce the district attorney of New Hampshire.

1846 Pierce joins the army as a private. He fights in the Mexican War as a brigadier general.

1848 Pierce leaves the army and returns to New Hampshire, disappointed that he had not proved to be a better soldier.

1850 Congress passes the Compromise of 1850.

1852 Pierce is nominated as the Democratic candidate for president. He is elected in November.

1853 Benjamin Pierce is killed in a train accident. Pierce is inaugurated the 14th president of the United States on March 4. Commodore Matthew Perry arrives in Japan, hoping to convince its leaders to begin trading with the United States. The Gadsden Purchase, in which the United States gains land in Arizona and New Mexico, is completed on December 30. This adds thousands of square miles to the nation. It also creates the border between the United States and Mexico.

1854 Commodore Perry and Japanese leaders sign a treaty to begin trade between the United States and Japan in March. Congress passes the Kansas-Nebraska Act in May. It says that people in those territories can decide whether to allow slavery. This angers many abolitionists, because the two territories were made free by the Missouri Compromise of 1820.

1856 Fighting breaks out in Kansas between abolitionists and supporters of slavery. John Brown and his followers attack and kill five pro-slavery men. Problems in Kansas grow so severe that 200 people are killed. People begin calling the territory "Bleeding Kansas." In May, Senator Charles Sumner gives an angry speech against slavery. Representative Preston Brooks from South Carolina severely beats Sumner on the Senate floor. The Democrats do not choose Pierce as their candidate for the next election. James Buchanan is elected the 15th president.

1857 Franklin Pierce leaves the presidency. He and Jane tour Europe, the West Indies, and the United States hoping to improve her health.

1859 John Brown and his followers attack the arsenal in Harper's Ferry, Virginia.

1860 Abraham Lincoln is elected president. Southern states begin to secede from the Union, fearing that he will abolish slavery. They found the Confederate States of America.

1861 The first shots are fired between the North and South at Fort Sumter in South Carolina on April 12. Throughout the Civil War, Pierce will speak out against Lincoln and the Union, claiming that they are to blame for the war.

1863 Jane Pierce dies on December 2.

1865 The Civil War ends. Abraham Lincoln is shot on April 14. He dies the next day.

1869 Franklin Pierce dies on October 8 in Concord, New Hampshire. He is buried with his wife and family at the Old North Cemetery in Concord.

abolish (uh-BAWL-ish)
If something is abolished, it is ended or made illegal. Pierce did not believe that slavery should be abolished.

abolitionists (ab-uh-LISH-uh-nists)
Abolitionists were people who wanted to end slavery before and during the Civil War. Pierce believed that both abolitionists and those in favor of slavery should be able to express their views.

ballots (BA-luts)
A ballot is a round of voting. It took 49 ballots for Democrats to nominate Pierce for their presidential candidate in 1852.

campaign (kam-PAYN)
A campaign is the process of running for an election, including activities such as giving speeches or attending rallies. Winfield Scott and his supporters said nasty things about Pierce during the presidential campaign of 1852.

candidate (KAN-duh-det)
A candidate is a person running in an election. The Democrats could not agree on a presidential candidate in 1852.

civil war (SIV-il WAR)
A civil war is a war between opposing groups of citizens from the same country or territory. A civil war broke out in Kansas between slaveholders and abolitionists.

constitution (kon-stih-TOO-shun)
A constitution is the set of basic principles that govern a state, country, or society. Pierce promised to protect states' rights that were guaranteed by the U.S. Constitution.

democracy (dee-MOK-reh-see)
A democracy is a country in which the government is run by the people who live there. Pierce and his father both believed in democracy.

federal (FED-ur-ul)
Federal means having to do with the central government of the United States, rather than a state or city government. The Democrats did not think the federal government should be too powerful.

**inauguration
(ih-nawg-yuh-RAY-shun)**
An inauguration is the ceremony that takes place when a new president begins a term. Pierce's inauguration took place on a gray, snowy day.

Glossary TERMS

nomination (NOM-ih-nay-shun)
If someone receives a nomination, he or she is chosen by a political party to run for an office. Pierce won the Democratic presidential nomination in 1852.

**political party
(puh-LIT-ih-kul PAR-tee)**
A political party is a group of people who share similar ideas about how to run a government. The Democratic Party is a political party.

politics (PAWL-uh-tiks)
Politics refers to the actions and practices of the government. Like his father, Pierce was interested in politics.

rebellion (reh-BEL-yen)
A rebellion is a fight against one's government. Pierce said the abolitionist government in Kansas was a form of rebellion.

representative (rep-ree-ZEN-tuh-tiv)
A representative is someone who attends a meeting, having agreed to speak or act for others. Pierce became a representative to the New Hampshire legislature in 1829.

revolution (rev-uh-LOO-shun)
A revolution is something that causes a complete change in government. The American Revolution was a war fought between the United States and Great Britain.

secede (suh-SEED)
If a group secedes, it separates from a larger group. Southern states began to secede from the Union after Abraham Lincoln was elected president.

territory (TAIR-uh-tor-ee)
A territory is a land or region, especially land that belongs to a government. Civil war broke out in the territory of Kansas in 1856.

traitor (TRAY-ter)
A traitor is someone who betrays his or her country. People accused Pierce of being a traitor when he talked badly about President Lincoln.

treaty (TREE-tee)
A treaty is a formal agreement between nations. Japan and the United States signed a treaty of friendship that opened trade between the two countries in 1854.

union (YOON-yen)
A union is the joining together of two people or groups of people, such as states. The Union is another name for the United States.

Our PRESENTS

President	Birthplace	Life Span	Presidency	Political Party	First Lady
George Washington	Virginia	1732–1799	1789–1797	None	Martha Dandridge Custis Washington
John Adams	Massachusetts	1735–1826	1797–1801	Federalist	Abigail Smith Adams
Thomas Jefferson	Virginia	1743–1826	1801–1809	Democratic-Republican	widower
James Madison	Virginia	1751–1836	1809–1817	Democratic Republican	Dolley Payne Todd Madison
James Monroe	Virginia	1758–1831	1817–1825	Democratic Republican	Elizabeth Kortright Monroe
John Quincy Adams	Massachusetts	1767–1848	1825–1829	Democratic-Republican	Louisa Johnson Adams
Andrew Jackson	South Carolina	1767–1845	1829–1837	Democrat	widower
Martin Van Buren	New York	1782–1862	1837–1841	Democrat	widower
William H. Harrison	Virginia	1773–1841	1841	Whig	Anna Symmes Harrison
John Tyler	Virginia	1790–1862	1841–1845	Whig	Letitia Christian Tyler / Julia Gardiner Tyler
James K. Polk	North Carolina	1795–1849	1845–1849	Democrat	Sarah Childress Polk

Our PRESIDENTS

President	*Birthplace*	Life Span	Presidency	Political Party	First Lady
Zachary Taylor	Virginia	1784–1850	1849–1850	Whig	Margaret Mackall Smith Taylor
Millard Fillmore	New York	1800–1874	1850–1853	Whig	Abigail Powers Fillmore
Franklin Pierce	New Hampshire	1804–1869	1853–1857	Democrat	Jane Means Appleton Pierce
James Buchanan	Pennsylvania	1791–1868	1857–1861	Democrat	never married
Abraham Lincoln	Kentucky	1809–1865	1861–1865	Republican	Mary Todd Lincoln
Andrew Johnson	North Carolina	1808–1875	1865–1869	Democrat	Eliza McCardle Johnson
Ulysses S. Grant	Ohio	1822–1885	1869–1877	Republican	Julia Dent Grant
Rutherford B. Hayes	Ohio	1822–1893	1877–1881	Republican	Lucy Webb Hayes
James A. Garfield	Ohio	1831–1881	1881	Republican	Lucretia Rudolph Garfield
Chester A. Arthur	Vermont	1829–1886	1881–1885	Republican	widower
Grover Cleveland	New Jersey	1837–1908	1885–1889	Democrat	Frances Folsom Cleveland

President	Birthplace	Life Span	Presidency	Political Party	First Lady
Benjamin Harrison	Ohio	1833–1901	1889–1893	Republican	Caroline Scott Harrison
Grover Cleveland	New Jersey	1837–1908	1893–1897	Democrat	Frances Folsom Cleveland
William McKinley	Ohio	1843–1901	1897–1901	Republican	Ida Saxton McKinley
Theodore Roosevelt	New York	1858–1919	1901–1909	Republican	Edith Kermit Carow Roosevelt
William H. Taft	Ohio	1857–1930	1909–1913	Republican	Helen Herron Taft
Woodrow Wilson	Virginia	1856–1924	1913–1921	Democrat	Ellen L. Axson Wilson Edith Bolling Galt Wilson
Warren G. Harding	Ohio	1865–1923	1921–1923	Republican	Florence Kling De Wolfe Harding
Calvin Coolidge	Vermont	1872–1933	1923–1929	Republican	Grace Goodhue Coolidge
Herbert C. Hoover	Iowa	1874–1964	1929–1933	Republican	Lou Henry Hoover
Franklin D. Roosevelt	New York	1882–1945	1933–1945	Democrat	Anna Eleanor Roosevelt Roosevelt
Harry S. Truman	Missouri	1884–1972	1945–1953	Democrat	Elizabeth Wallace Truman

Our PRESIDENTS

President	Birthplace	Life Span	Presidency	Political Party	First Lady
Dwight D. Eisenhower	Texas	1890–1969	1953–1961	Republican	Mary "Mamie" Doud Eisenhower
John F. Kennedy	Massachusetts	1917–1963	1961–1963	Democrat	Jacqueline Bouvier Kennedy
Lyndon B. Johnson	Texas	1908–1973	1963–1969	Democrat	Claudia Alta Taylor Johnson
Richard M. Nixon	California	1913–1994	1969–1974	Republican	Thelma Catherine Ryan Nixon
Gerald Ford	Nebraska	1913–	1974–1977	Republican	Elizabeth "Betty" Bloomer Warren Ford
James Carter	Georgia	1924–	1977–1981	Democrat	Rosalynn Smith Carter
Ronald Reagan	Illinois	1911–	1981–1989	Republican	Nancy Davis Reagan
George Bush	Massachusetts	1924–	1989–1993	Republican	Barbara Pierce Bush
William Clinton	Arkansas	1946–	1993–2001	Democrat	Hillary Rodham Clinton
George W. Bush	Connecticut	1946–	2001–	Republican	Laura Welch Bush

Presidential FACTS

Qualifications

To run for president, a candidate must
- be at least 35 years old
- be a citizen who was born in the United States
- have lived in the United States for 14 years

Term of Office

A president's term of office is four years. No president can stay in office for more than two terms.

Election Date

The presidential election takes place every four years on the first Tuesday of November.

Inauguration Date

Presidents are inaugurated on January 20.

Oath of Office

I do solemnly swear I will faithfully execute the office of the President of the United States and will to the best of my ability preserve, protect, and defend the Constitution of the United States.

Write a Letter to the President

One of the best things about being a U.S. citizen is that Americans get to participate in their government. They can speak out if they feel government leaders aren't doing their jobs. They can also praise leaders who are going the extra mile. Do you have something you'd like the president to do? Should the president worry more about the environment and encourage people to recycle? Should the government spend more money on our schools? You can write a letter to the president to say how you feel!

1600 Pennsylvania Avenue
Washington, D.C. 20500

You can even send an e-mail to: president@whitehouse.gov

For Further INFORMATION

Internet Sites

Read a biography about President Pierce from the Encyclopedia Britannica:
http://www.britannica.com/bcom/eb/article/4/0,5716,61474+1,00.html

Read information on Franklin Pierce's boyhood home:
http://www.conknet.com/~hillsboro/historic/homestead.html

Visit the house where Franklin Pierce lived after leaving the Senate and before going to the Mexican War:
http://www.newww.com/free/pierce/pierce.html

Read Nathaniel Hawthorne's biography of Franklin Pierce:
http://eldred.ne.mediaone.net/nh/lfp.html

Read President Grant's obituary for Franklin Pierce:
http://starship.python.net/crew/manus/Presidents/fp/fpobit.html

Visit two links to sites about Franklin Pierce:
http://www.geocities.com/CapitolHill/Lobby/5296/pres_franklin_pierce.html
http://www.interlink-cafe.com/uspresidents/14th.htm

Learn more about all the presidents and visit the White House:
http://www.whitehouse.gov/WH/glimpse/presidents/html/presidents.html
http://www.thepresidency.org/presinfo.htm
http://www.americanpresidents.org

Books

Blassingame, Wyatt. *The Look-It-Up Book of Presidents.* New York: Random House, 1984.

Feinberg, Barbara Silberdick. *America's First Ladies.* New York: Franklin Watts, 1998.

Ochoa, George. *The Fall of Mexico City.* Englewood Cliffs, NJ: Silver Burdett Press, 1989.

Smith, Carter. *Presidents of a Young Republic.* Brookfield, CT: Millbrook Press, 1993.

Rubel, David. *The United States in the 19th Century.* New York: Scholastic, 1996.

Index